Pulse

By Natasha Head

Winter Goose
Publishing

Winter Goose Publishing
2701 Del Paso Road, 130-92
Sacramento, CA 95835

www.wintergoosepublishing.com
Contact Information: info@wintergoosepublishing.com

Pulse

COPYRIGHT © 2013 by Natasha Head

First Edition, March 2013

ISBN: 978-0-9889049-5-8

Cover Art by Winter Goose Publishing
Typeset by Michelle Lovi

Published in the United States of America

To the girl who never was and all she'd dreamt she'd be . . .

Table of Contents

Road Kill

Night Shift

His eyes were tired.
Two a.m.
Dark road, corn field trim,
and a double-shift at the mill.

Lost the farm
but not the memories,
nor the shame that came with it.
Mind elsewhere,
eyes elsewhere.
Dancing across the yellow line.
No one was there to see.

The stone-washed asphalt darkened.
His mind could not comprehend,
a shadow, yet solid,
on the edge of the golden glare.

It was just dumb luck,
he realized.
It was something more than shadow.

A black lump in the road.
Was it even worth swerving?
He laughed . . .
The way his luck had been lately,
it wasn't a chance he was willing to take.

He brought the old Ford to a slow rolling stop.
Crickets sang into the darkness.
Somewhere,
lost amongst the rows of corn,
a bullfrog sounded,
but . . .
it was the eerie call of the loon
that gave him the shivers.

He was a grown man
not prone to think twice
about things that go bump in the night,
or shadows without explanation . . .

Even with his headlights
spotlighting the form,
he didn't know what he was looking at.

Another day
coming up a dollar short,
he had other things on his mind.

His steel-toed boots landed heavy
on the cracked and splintered asphalt.
His shadow grew before him
as he moved into the surreal glow of the headlights.
The steady running engine
purring a backdrop to the loons.

The closer he came to the form
the closer he came to realization.

A bare foot.
A leg that was never meant to bend that way.
The black path leading to the pool
that in the flood of light
could no longer deny the red . . .

His gag reflex engaged.
He barked into the night
as he fell to his knees,
praying for pulse.

Flatline

1

Current Events from a Day Just Remembered

She smiled.
It had been a long time
since June was hot enough
to invite all skin.

He hated tan lines,
always had.
For once she was able
to forgo the interior baking
offered up in the rear
of Jerry's Pizza
for a buck a minute.

Besides . . . if he came home early
she'd be quick to appear ready and waiting.
He liked that.

The steady thud she had been trying to ignore
grew louder,
despite Green Day blaring
"Another turning point . . ."
She hummed along
like she always did.
Like he always hated.

But he wasn't due home for hours,
and the house and yard were hers.

Still, the steady thud.
Stomp . . . stomp . . . stomp . . .
Haunted House footsteps,
no explanation.

No matter.
More construction,
more road work,
causing more damage
than was being fixed.
Hell bound
on keeping the blue collared
where they belonged.

She lay, cat-like,
stretching her naked form,
accepting of the sun's kiss.

Stomp . . . stomp . . . stomp . . .

Baking in the June sun
of a surreal afternoon.

Stomp . . . stomp . . . stomp . . .

In the little piece of suburbia
no one admitted to.

Just on the fringe of the haves
where have-not housewives
were really two-dollar whores,
and time was paid for by the minute.

"Time takes you by the wrist . . ."

Stomp . . . stomp . . . stomp . . .

She took a pull from the bottle of beer
she snuck from the Thursday night 2-4.
He wouldn't mind;
today was something special.
Hell . . . they had waited all year.

They had learned long ago,
if he was drinking
she wasn't.
These days . . .
it seemed he never stopped.

The beer was cold,
the bottle sweating,
and it felt so good going down.
She closed her eyes,
savoring every sip,
until a shadow covered the sun.

She had no idea who he was
but the boots.
Slasher psychotics wore boots like that.
She opened her mouth to scream,
and somehow
. . . suddenly
. . . . . . slipped.

Witness

By the Wrist

It was there . . . but it was feint.
His mind raced.
His body faster
to the top of the hill for a signal,
while she lay
broken,
bleeding,
barely
breathing.

He swore he could hear his heart
pumping adrenalin
somewhere outside of his body.

Goosebumps.
Hair standing on end,
despite the still humid air
of a disappearing
summer-night skyline.

Large, dumb fingers
shaking.
Tiny smartphone buttons,
numb.
Work made him carry it:
on-call
twenty-four/seven.

He screamed out loud,
cursing the god
he had only moments before
been praying to.

Suddenly . . .
Finally . . .
Connection . . .

And seconds
turned to hours,
turned to dawn.

They wouldn't let him leave.
Uniforms and shiny badges.
Top rank.
The law.

Questions.
Questions.
More fucking questions.
Frayed nerves.
No sleep.
Hands in hair,
desperation near.

Finally, just a moment
to breathe.

She was young.
She was beautiful,

but she was oh so very broken.

Sometimes grown men cry,
when dawn is nearing
and they are close to breaking.
Sometimes they really
have no other choice.

So now he sat,
bone to solid asphalt,
head in hands,
while about him
the lights rolled,
the voices carried,
and a life
just barely
held on.

Flatline
II

Cause for Concern

Oh, how he loved Thirsty Thursday . . .
drunk before dinner,
one proud dirty sinner,
warming up for the days ahead.

She squinted her eyes . . .
a strobing red pulsed around her,
vibrating,
rolling the molars,
ringing her ears.

Flashback now:
another time,
another place.
When dance steps meant dollars
and private "conversations."

Bottle after bottle
she continued her chore.
No cold beer would mean bruises that night.
Still the pulse, pulse, pulse,
of the red, red, red.
Must have been something she said.
Never mind
the drip, drip, drip,
of the red, red, red.

She should have called her mother.
She needed to talk to her mother.
She had been bad.
She had kept secrets.
The sudden need for confession
overwhelmed her,
even though
she knew it was her mother
who needed it more.

Mother would be no good here.
Mother could not breathe here.
No chance to say good-bye.
No chance for forgiveness.
Only judgement,
only fear.
No love.
Pulsing.

He was playing Sabbath again
"Finished with my woman cause she . . ."
She shook her head
ignoring the drip, drip, drip.
He loved that song,
knew there was no help for his mind
and made no excuses about it.

With cold beer in hand,
condensation
silky against her skin.

Bottle cold
to hot neck.
Tip toe
to the bedroom.
On route,

she simply slipped . . .

Mentor

"You know . . . boys are different than girls."
A familiar voice.
Mature, husky.
The yellow of nicotine,
the stains on the fingers.
Despite the diamond
decorations.
False teeth
gleaming between lying red lips.

Her eyes rolled.
She couldn't remember.

"They're needy. You have to know how
to take care of 'em."

Hulling beans
fresh from the garden,
waiting for Grandmother's return.

Grandmother.
Naïve,
unassuming,
as much of the problem.
Swimming in denial . . .
Eyes wide-open,
but blind.

"And you gotta be able to put up with their shit
if you ever plan on keeping one."

Aunt Jane,
in from the city.
Long nails,
red lips.
She smelled of money
and something else.

"I want to be like Jane."
The innocence of the young,
soon to be gone.
Her grandmother would scold her.
Sometimes even slap her.
Seems no one thought as highly of Jane
as she.

If Jane was so bad
then why was she allowed to stay?
Was it the black eyes and bruises
that made them feel guilty?

She could remember now
that Jane didn't always look so hot,
no matter how many drug store runs she made,
no matter how thick the face paint,
there was always something about Jane.

Spoke like a trucker,
smoked like a chimney,

and liked her liquor
straight from the bottle.

"You need a man in this world, little lady."
Lips pucker, drawing on cigarette.
"The world don't take well to folks like us.
If you can find one with money,
lots of it,
you'll have a better life."
Life lessons from Jane.

Lady Jane

Wednesday.
Bingo night at the fire hall.
Grandma insisted on chips,
cursing the ink-filled dobbers
her shaky hands
couldn't manage.
Called a false bingo
once
and near died from embarrassment.

Jane was always so quick to shuffle her out the door,
carpooling grey hairs
off for a night of adventure.

Grandma never knew what Wednesdays really meant to her.
When Jane would take her upstairs,
rolling her hair,
powdering her nose,
but only after a scalding cleanse
in the old claw footed tub . . .
Cleanliness is next to godliness,
she would smile,
and real men appreciated a woman
who knew how to keep herself ready.

Twelve years old
in high heels
and a little black dress

brought in from the big city.
Her growing breasts clinched tight,
spilling over the drop neck.

She never knew how good she looked
until Jane's friends arrived,
all smiles and drug store aftershave.

One fool arrived with flowers.
How Jane laughed
as she threw them on the table
amongst Grandma's knick-knacks,
but took the bills
and buried them in her own ample bosom.

How it had hurt,
those rough hands
venturing to those places
even she dared not go,
no matter the desire that was born
in the hours after dark.

But worse,
so much worse
was the sound.
The haggard breathing.
The nasty words.
Hair pulled.
Head shoved.
And the smell.

Always finished
before Grandma returned.
Our secret.
Jane would smile,
tossing her a crumpled
twenty dollar bill
with the promise of better days ahead.

Jane knew the ways of the world
and knew it wasn't always pretty,
but there was nothing you couldn't handle
if you had a man with money.

Men to Boys

Watermelon.
Hot July.
The smell.
The pink flesh dripping
over the chest
of Brady Gray.
Sixteen,
and so much smoother than Jane's friends.

He spoke of love
with a twinkle in his eye,
spitting the large black seeds.
Proud of his distance.

Her first official conquest.
No help from Jane.
He brought her comic books and candy
in exchange for stolen moments
at the ball field dug outs.

Brady would never have much more than the candy to offer
but made for the sweetest of teachers
not knowing all she knew.
Thinking he was the leader.
Taking her hand.
Placing it in forbidden places.
Dreaming forbidden dreams.

She remembered the watermelon.
His skin sticky.
The rough back of the ball park bench
digging into her
while he made promises
for all their tomorrows

She remembered
knowing his words
were no different
than those
breathed hot into her ear,
formed by the lips of men
who made those same vows
to women who would never know their secrets.

Falling now,
through the marshmallow clouds
that promised the world
through the chain-link
of the back stop.

. . . rough hands
. . . grabbing hold
. . . bruising shoulders
. . . pulling her up.

Family

Mama

The gurney busted through the swinging doors.
Flapping in the rush of power,
bodies danced about the bed,
men and women
urging her return.

Vials, tubes.
Bones broken.
Body bleeding.
Eating the blood of another.
Survival
at the hands of white jackets
and unknown doners.

A small, grey haired woman,
eyes red,
jumps to her feet.
She wears her long stringy hair
in a convoluted bun
pinned to the top of her tiny head.
Her eyes,
bloodshot pin holes
in white sunken skin.

"My baby!"
Her scream so sincere.
Looking to see if anyone noticed.
"This is my baby, my sweet baby!"

Eyes dart about the sterile hallway.
Alligator tears dry quickly
when she sees no one is listening.

A white-coated man,
clipboard in hand,
takes her arm.

Contact made
from an age-old student id
tracked down through systems.
The information highway.
Big Brother knows his stuff.

"When was the last time you saw your daughter?"
His eyes are kind, his voice soft,
but there is no mistaking his authority.

"Why the fuck is that any of your business?
You a cop?"
Voice stern, gravelly,
already suspicious.
Outside her comfort zone
where answers were mandatory.
She needed a cigarette.
Look of surprise
in doctors' eyes.

"A bit of information . . .
Could lead to a clue
of what we're dealing with,
how we can help her."

The snort that responded
was not that of concerned caretaker.
"She was strolling stoned again?
Is that what you're trying to tell me?
Too interested in flying higher
to notice? What would you think, Doc,
if they found your daughter like that, eh?
Not even enough decency
to roll her to the side?"

The gurney now gone
through two more doors.
Emergency.
Flapping in the wind.
Left behind by the people
fighting to save her daughter's life.

"I need a cigarette."
Doc stared after her.

Charitable Donations

"Some fucking father you turned out to be!"
The voice screamed through the night at him.
Across roadways.
Pavement.
Dragging the wasted body
behind it.

He stared at the raging woman before him.
She brought her handbag down,
slamming it against the side
of the Lexus he had just stepped from.

"Where is she?"
His voice calm,
his wisdom knowing.
The conversation would not end well.

For twenty years
he had never known.
The guilt consumed him.

For twenty years,
his baby,
left to the vision of insanity
that now stormed at him.

"Where is she? Where is SHE?
Where the fuck where you?"

He pushed past her,
pulse racing,
head reeling.

Near death,
country road,
almost dawn.
He was suddenly existing
within a novel he had never written.

No one would answer his questions.
Perhaps no one could.

Cracked red leather seat
against the lime green walls,
waiting in the aroma
of antiseptic.

A daughter.
A father to a twenty-three-year-old
ADULT.
No baby steps,
no family memories.
Just the baggage
his absence had caused.

Protocol

The boys in blue with questions for you.
She could taste the blood.
Tongue bitten.
Who the hell were they to question,
the life she had provided?
Done all she could.
Kept her fed,
a roof over her head.

Look at him;
middle-aged,
well–to-do.
Hard to believe
he one time fucked you . . .

She sneered into the face of the officer.
"She lived with her boyfriend."
"Sycamore and Cherry."
"Twenty-three . . . she's twenty-three years old.
I don't watch every fucking move!"

Raging again.
Not caring who saw.
The man who found her
turned away when their eyes met.
More blood, as she bit her tongue again.
He could have left her,
avoided all this . . .

Now Daddy to the rescue,
clutching her arm,
pulling her back.

Her fierce eyes glared.
"I'm contagious . . . it's called welfare."
He rolled his eyes.
"This isn't your pity party, Sara."

He turned back to the officer,
tone apologetic,
she was sick of him already.

Flatline
III

Faith

There was blackness surrounding her now.
Clogging orifices,
pouring from her eyes,
embalmed in shadow.

Life force black.
Swimming.
Swimming.
Like fowl through oil slicks
on broadcast news,
her wings were heavy.

"Jesus saves."
She cringed away from the voice,
too familiar.
Sinking deeper into the forgotten pew.
Gagging on the scent.
Old bibles.
Incense.

Not seeing
cold against her body.
Sliding.
Caressing.

"God created man
in his own image . . .
You are an abomination

thus cursed to bleed
when no man will lay with you."

She had been seeking salvation.
He had been seeking other things.

The family name
had made it to the church
long before she ever did.

Hot whispers in her ears,
tongues of devils,
licking, splitting.
He had told her she had the voice of an angel,
promised saving,
forgiveness,
a ticket to the pearly gates,
earned on her knees.
Like so many sticky school boys
at the mercy of desire . . .

Her pulse ringing,
slow, steady,
in the darkness,
she found fear.
But in the blood she found peace.

A candle in the window
of a childhood home.
Known
for but a moment.

Pulsing.
Calling to her.
The only light she saw.
The only memory she never wanted to lose.

She swam harder.

Abandoned

"It's just for a little while, babe.
I'll be back before you know it."
Her mother's voice.
Cold, as it always was.
The first time
she had been forced to really see her
for all the hate she represented.

The hug was for the sake of the woman in the skirt suit,
even at ten years old she was smart enough to know that.

The feel of her grandmother's rough hand
firm on her side as she pulled her close
into the scent of Avon parties and Tupperware
and the stale smoke of the bingo hall.

"You've got your own room here,
and Jane's coming home too.
You Love Jane."

Mother . . . too stupid to realize
how much more Jane loved her
and the payroll she would come to provide.

Racoon eyes pleading
as the officer pushed her head down,
forcing her into the cruiser.
Blue and red lights pulsing.

Pulsing . . . pulsing.

The suit cases came next.
A matching set.
Stinking.
Up from the depth of the cellar
where Sal would never let her go.

This was his house, the last she would ever know as home,
but Sal never returned.

Her mother couldn't have known,
but she would do the time just the same . . .

Those yellow suitcases had haunted for years.
The crusty, rusty streaks.
The money.
For so long such a burden,
now in ample supply.

No one would answer her questions,
save for Jane . . .
All too happy to fill in the blanks
of a story that never should have been told.

Coming Round

Her heart was on fire
Flames blinding
As she was pulled back from the light
Shadows exploding
Into a thousand shards
Electricity
Suddenly alive
Blood magnetic

The sound
Her blood pulsing
Intensified
Alive
A voice
Right in her ear
"We've got her
Hold ON!"

Fighting the volts
Clinging to shadows
Resistance . . .
Futile

Mechanical Gods
Calling her back

Ghosts dancing
Fingers caressing

Yellow lines
Black tar
Smoking tires
Burning
Into the horizon . . .

The Moments
in
Between

Savior

He stared back and forth.
Her, crazy as a loon.
Him, embarrassed.
And him left standing between the two.

Black coffee.
Thick,
bitter,
not caring.
Disgusted by the display
of selfish humanity before him.

Feet pulsing.
He had to sit.
Work would be upon him again.
Not long after a lunch
that would never be served.

A night-long vigil
of deep breaths,
silent prayers
for a broken stranger
who had more than the asphalt to blame.

With no division between the dark and dawn,
his mind still fought the images.
The matted blonde curls,
crimson ringlets.

Bouncing onto the white linens
of an ambulance gurney.

No words,
but for an instant
her eyes had met his.
Staring back at him
through a distance too far away to be measured.

That look
still holding him frozen
throughout the questioning.

Throughout the foolish banter
of the crazy woman,
the poor girl called mother.

Throughout the shame and embarrassment
washing across the face of her father.

The girl was alone.
No matter how many bodies
lined up to pray,
only the devil
could hear them.

"Sara, stop, please."
His face was red.
Rage?
Perhaps.
"How was I supposed to know?
You think I'd want MY daughter

being raised by the likes of you
and your fucked up family?"

For once the woman was silent.

Hate,
pure and unadulterated,
pulsed in her gaze.
Frail, tiny hands,
curling, slowly
into fists.

She was on him,
beating,
clawing.
Blood welled
as her nails made contact,
pulling trails of flesh behind them.
Nurses came running,
doctors came running.
She was filled with the strength
of every broken promise
the world had dealt her.

Pulsing.
Coursing through her veins.
He let her win.
Never raised a hand in his own defence.
Took the blows like a champ,
but couldn't quite hide the tears
that pooled in the corners of his eyes.

"Mr. Atwater . . .
you can see her now."
He shot one last look
as security continued to drag
a former one night stand
down the long, sick-lit hallway.

The stranger watched silently.
The woman,
the man,
forever connected
in the blood of conception.
Forever fighting
the worth of the consequence.

The broken angel
would only always remind them
of wrong turns
and bad decisions,
and he knew
a parent's love
she had never known.

Lost Time

She was a barely breathing lump among many.
ICU.
Over populated,
under funded.
Too old to realize the benefits
that came with her father's money.

Awake, alive.
She had been beautiful,
if tired.
He remembered his first look,
the resemblance.
So much more than coincidence would allow.

Golden blonde curls.
Eyes the fiercest of greens,
yet somehow
ancient,
lost in a face that
was so much harder than her years
should have allowed.

She was tough, this one.
With over twenty years
of her mother's lies,
like poison
already abloom
in her heart.

For the first time
now
he gazed upon the little girl
he had never known.

Tears.
Alone.
No wrath of the wicked woman
still being held captive outside.
They were tears of shame,
remembering how
upon his first glance
the urge to run
had almost overcome.

Too easy to deny
the seed of a woman
who made her way in the world,
legs spread,
ready to collect the coins
from any who held her fortune.

He himself
had been so young.
A college prank
for one who
just wanted to get the whole thing
. . . over with.

For over twenty years
he thought he had . . .

A secret that would travel to his grave,
blown wide open
on a sheet of paper
from a cheap drugstore notebook
delivered to his wife
on an evening
when he was once again
working late . . .

Holed up in his little room
above their three-car garage.
Bought and paid for
on imagined nightmares
and the desire to scare
now all too real . . .

He took her hand,
and there,
beneath the pale skin
bruised from tubes
sustaining her heart,
he felt her
sleeping,
but alive.

He held the hand
just like that,
for as long as they would let him,
feeling her life
so new to him.

Now,
so dangerously close
to losing,
after all the battles,
the explanations,
the skeletons dancing
out of their dusty closets.
Too little too late
to make a difference.

Envy

She refused to enter
until they made him leave.
White collar
piece of shit.

Writing tales of adventure
from lake cabin shores.
Raising daughters worthy of his name.

She laughed out loud,
ignoring the surprised looks
on the faces of the others
who waited.

A discount for a first-timer.
How stupid she had been,
accepting a drink afterward.
Only wanting to feel
like she was wanted,
not bought for an hour
and forgotten.

He was a good kid
and she had hated him for it,
knowing she would never
follow through with her plan.

The seed took,
unlike all the times before,
but the little bit of false pride
she could still cling to
would not let her express her need.

So she had done what she could alone . . .
Now, staring down at the form
that had stolen so much of her own life,
the taste of resentment,
the sting of envy.

Her baby
could have been anything she had wanted,
if only they would have let her believe.
She reached out
to grasp the same hand
that only moments before
had been released
by the man she now knew as father
. . . but she couldn't bring herself to do it.

She knew she should be feeling something,
and maybe,
somewhere in the dark twisted garden of her heart,
she was . . .

But she could not name the relief
until she was sure the life
had truly stopped . . .

There was no life worth saving,
that slumbered,
medicated,
inebriated,
on morphine dreams,
for once legitimate.

Her prayers were of a different sort.
For new beginnings,
for fresh starts.
So much like
the daughter
she had resented
every single day
of her pathetic existence.

For the first time in over twenty years,
she could finally imagine
a clean slate.

Flatline
IV

Sal

How he had laughed with them.
Group hugs and ice cream cones.
Giving them a home
when no one else would.

The smell of burgers
on the grill.
REAL burgers.
Not frozen patties from food-bank freezers.

The scent of chlorine on the breeze
as they readied the pool.
THEIR pool.
Taking up most of the rolling-back lawn,
peppered with poppies and lupins.
Who knew
she'd be transplanted before the chemical cocktail was
deemed safe.

Those long Saturday afternoons
when he'd let her watch movies,
sitting on his lap,
hands under blankets
while mother was working.

Our secret,
he'd whisper,
and she somehow

thought he'd meant
the rating of the movie . . .

Her hand,
suddenly warmer now.
Silky, wet.

Just another accident
to hide from mother.

How she had cried when he left.
How she had longed for his return.
What had she done?

Alone again.
Stuck in the little ranch-style bungalow
in a town neither her nor her mother knew.
Where no friends could visit
until they did something about the smell.
Where no curtains could be opened,
no matter the sunshine.
And no lights,
save for the entrance,
after dark . . .

With him went the money
and any semblance of normal she had ever known.

They had held on,
watching the cupboards grow bare.
And she had hid in the evenings,

like mother instructed.
Steering clear
of the basement,
like she had promised Sal she would.

Praying, if she was good enough
he would return.

There is nothing worse
than waiting in the dark,
no distraction,
alone.
Mother trying her best
and she
ducked low
in the furthest corner
of a forgotten closet
where she was safe to shine the flashback
on ancient magazines
and little golden books
where she would realize
there was no such thing as fairy tales,
and princes never stayed.

The Truth According to Jane

Driving through with Grandmother.
Dirt road,
after dark.
Chasing the shadow of the old station wagon.
Bouncing headlights,
fear.

Mother carted off.
The silver glean of the handcuffs
haunting her sleep
as she was folded into a yellow suitcase
whose interior bled red.

The house had never belonged to Sal,
Jane was quick to inform,
he was just lucky enough
to know that
no one would miss the crotchety old bachelor
stored in the basement.

No one noticed the difference
in the signatures
on the pension checks
that went right on being cashed.
Why would they?

The man had had no family,
no friends,

was more than willing to accept
the companionship
of a bright young out-of-towner
down on his luck.

Until Jane,
she had no idea the life they had been living
had been stolen.

An image of a man,
a good man,
wafted in her mind
just out of reach.

But Rod wouldn't shut up.
Electric guitars and rock star dreams,
bought and paid for
on street corners.
Hour long motels,
studio time,
funded by a tight ass
and breasts that defied gravity.

His sleaze-bag stare,
through a haze of smoke,
somehow confused with love.
Somewhere
her own laughter,
so much like her mother's,
pulsed within her mind.

He'd never have the chance
to come rubbing up on her like that again . . .

Why did they have to take Mom away?
Back with her grandmother now,
bumping down the dirt road
to the old clap-board house
where the ancient oak
was home to a tire swing
that let her fly high enough to touch the sky.

Grandmother never answered,
no matter how she prodded.
Eyes on the road,
hands tight to the wheel.
Cigarette smoke
curling through the rollers
that never left her hair,
save for bingo night and church.

But Jane had the answers.
Her mother was stupid,
always had been.
Letting the boys run her
instead of the other way around.

Sal was a no good, coke snorting fiend
that needed a decent whore to fund his habit.
Mother never had class like Jane,
and thank Sweet Jesus she got here in time
to keep her off the same path . . .

Class in session.
Black patent stilettos.
Fish-net.
The proper walk.
The sexy swing.

You could train a man, you know.
It just took a little practice . . .

Front row.
Center stage.
Spotlight shining.

One hit wonder.
Video dancer.
The money didn't last,
only the lifestyle it fostered.

Return to the corner.
A has-been at twenty-three.
Rode hard,
played crooked.
Karma's cruel joke.

But the men always believed in her,
in whatever she allowed them to perceive her to be.

Jane had provided the roles.
Open-ended scripts.
Leaving room for compromise,
but no room for who she really was.

Betrayed

Brady came from a good family,
one that knew better
than to be seen with the likes of her's,
yet he never let her know that . . .

He made her feel like a lady.
He was gentle,
easy.
But he hated Jane . . .

The pulse of watermelon pink.
She thought maybe she could have loved him.
Walking home,
after dark,
under the canopy of branches
that umbrella her road.
Never allowed to take his daddy's car on the dirt,
he always made the walk with her.

He knew where her mother was.
She had confessed to him
under a pregnant July moon
after he had enough.
Laid back against the trunk of the tire-swing oak,
holding her like no one else would ever be able to.

He was smart.
Really smart.

He read books, sometimes to her,
recited poetry
in fake accent,
but most of all he warned against Jane
until mother returned . . .
and Jane was suddenly forgotten.

As the moon crossed the sky
towards the end of July,
Mother reclaimed her room
and sent Jane packing,
and her life suddenly
became dull . . .

Tending to a lush,
making excuses,
feeling the need to run,
to be someone.
Found again
in the arms of strangers
who liked the way she danced,
willing to pay for romance.
Taking bingo night to the streets,
never home before Grandma,
with one glaring exception.

Heart split in two
at the sight.
Him—embarrassed.
Her—smug.
Him, grabbing clothes from the floor.

Her, lying naked on her daughter's bed.
No shame.
She felt the break,
knew a piece of her had died.
Mother never spoke of it
and Brady never came back.

Forgive and forget,
whispered Jane
from a distant memory.
Sweet tea on the back patio
that was never really
anything more than
boards from a dying barn.
A sawed-off oil barrel
fire-pit.
Hell flames
licking.
No forgiveness will ever be found
in a heart betrayed
by mother.

Never Say Die

Alone in the black.
Alone in the world.
But there was daddy,
somewhere.
Not useless.
Not deadbeat.

Suddenly the stories her mother had told
didn't quite match up.
Mother was not well,
never was.
Mother never loved
anyone more than she had loved herself.

The blackness engulfed her
as per her invitation.
Cordially,
lovingly
she became embraced,
caressed,
full
for the first time
ever.

She resonated with its pulse,
and suddenly
all the pain she had fought to forget
rushed at her

out of the darkness.
Grating,
scraping,
tearing through the blackness of never
to
always-will-be.

And now more than blackness pulsed.
Rage,
brilliant,
colorful,
alive,
burst into the black,
igniting will,
desire.
Pure,
beautifully frightening
anger.
It would NOT
end this way.

Beneath the still white sheet
a body came to life.
Movement,
with no one round
to notice.

Awakening

Hello Mother

Lips, drawn.
Lacking the smile
that brightened shadows
in spite of it all.

Pale, gray, and waxen.
The golden crown of golden locks
now stood lopsided.
The bruising hidden by soft stubble
simply not strong enough to support its kingdom.

Sara's tired, age-spotted hand
caressed a cheek
that offered no warmth,
no rosy glow
in spite of it all . . .

Who would leave her baby
beaten and bleeding
on asphalt that
seldom saw the rubber
of the road?

The quiet lips
suddenly parted at her touch.
soft breath
exhaled across her barely feeling skin.

Fear overtook her.
She jumped back
away from her "baby."
She had all but said her goodbyes.

The still form spasomed,
sat bolt upright,
and turned her head.

Mute-Hated

The voices were soft,
fearful of being overheard.
She stayed silent
through it all.

Mute . . . she played with the term in her mind.
"As a result of the impact."
That worked.

Eyes shut against the light pouring through the blinds.
Ears wide open.
Pacing breath
to ensure safe passage.

"What do you mean you don't know?
How can you not fucking know?!"

She fought to hide her smile.
The loving tone of her mother.
Never missed, never to be missed again.

"Sara . . . she's sleeping.
Keep your voice down,
please."

Yes . . . there it was.
The voice of the one who could help her.
Who owed her . . .

sanctuary?
She supposed so.

But all those years lost?
No sense of obligation
beyond the guilt
that shadowed his spirit.

She was not "Mother."
She needed no "Father."
She would not stumble
blind to doorsteps
where her presence
was a crime
and her worth
could be bought.

The Event

The steady beeping of the machines
still connected.
Her head aching
. . . but she figured that would have to be expected.

When she had purposely jumped from the cab of his truck,
there was never to be any waking.

His was a hand who had yet to lay upon her.
No surprise there.
More concerned
with protecting the garden,
laying low.

At the back of her mind,
still forming,
she could say he pushed her,
call it her last laugh.
But that would take the last of her.
More than she was willing to give.

As she feigned sleep
she felt the future began to unfold.

"She will need time to sort through,
time to remember . . ."

"What are you saying?"
Her mother again.
Like the sad, lost little girl
she always was . . .

"Your daughter has experienced a major blow.
There will need to be x-rays, assessments . . .
The fact she's awake and moving,
it's a miracle in itself."

"Of course she's fucking moving!"
The return of the witch.
"It's killing her being strapped like that.
Trust me . . . I know my girl."

"She's not strapped, Ms. Cochrane.
Those are simply connections for us to track her vitals.
The three broken bones in her leg
will be enough to keep her from moving."
This time there was a tone of impatience.
The doctor was tiring of fighting with a woman
who had no chance of seeing reason . . .

Moving gray slid across her eyelids.
Still she remained.
No seeing.
The cold bony hand of her mother
ensnared her own,
the insincerity
palpable.

The Watchmen

Nighttime in a hospital
where nightmares roam corridors
and the screaming never stops.

They wanted to watch,
keep an eye on her . . .
She still refused to speak,
and was content to let them call it
medical.
Vocal chords fine,
all in her mind . . .

Nightlights and gilded hallways.
Police officers
still content to leave her be for now.
But how much longer?

Other mothers,
real mothers,
crying out.

A lover's rage.
A son's first car accident.
A robbery gone wrong.
But no one had yet figured out
what happened to the
beautiful mute
in room 115 . . .

Just three doors down
from emergency,
from triage,
where her silence kept her
front of mind.

Progress

Days dragging.
Hair growing back.
Leg on the mend.
Three places.
White cast.
A mother and a father
determined to have the biggest signature.

They didn't know
if she knew them.
They didn't know
if she understood.
But in floating through the ether
she somehow got smart,
and unwilling to share her secrets.

The police invaded.
Day thirteen.
Surprise.
They were big,
they were young,
they were still looking
for the man that did this to her.

She widened her green eyes.
A look of innocence,
of confusion.
Pleading ignorance
without saying a word.

They left quick enough,
obviously frustrated.
She wasn't used to sending men away like that.

Toys of her youth
lined up beside her.
Her mother all but begging
for an ounce,
one iota of a sign,
that maybe she would remember.

There was Sam,
the yorkie terrier pup.
Filthy, mauled,
bought by Sal,
and she thought this would be a good thing.

She resisted lashing out at the woman before her,
kept her expression clueless
and tried to ignore the pain
on fire in her heart.

Her mother never knew.
Her mother never would.

He was handsome,
awkward.
There was no questioning
who was the daddy . . .
He was miserable.
She could see it in his eyes.

He had never asked for this,
had never known.

She couldn't hate him
'cause he had always been playing the game
from a default position.

He hugged her everyday.
Smiled, despite his pain.
Told her stories of his youth,
took it as an opportunity for her to know him better.
Starting from scratch,
like he thought they were.

She supposed he considered this
some sort of blessing.
A memory of hate and abuse
wiped clean.
And she knew they figured it was by
more abuse
that she came to be here.
Self-inflicted . . . they would never know.

There were days when she wanted to speak,
to smile and say "fooling"
like she used to do with her mom,
until Aunt Jane mocked her . . .

She wanted her daddy,
more now than ever,
but understood

that time was passed.
There was no room in her plan
for close ties and connection.

There was,
for the first time in her life,
only room for her.

For the first time,
she finally understood
"courage"
was not surviving a life on the streets.
"Courage"
was not bouncing back
after being beaten.
"Courage"
was knowing
she deserved better
and demanding from life
she get it.

Rod

He came to her on day twenty-one,
after everyone
had given up hope
of normal ever returning.

Hot Rod.
She couldn't help
the look of recognition
that danced across her face.
He was too stoned to notice.

She could smell him,
her senses alive in sobriety.
How did she live with it . . .
He knew what she had done,
not that anyone believed him.
She heard them talking.
He wasn't here for her,
he was here to save himself . . .

"Look, Doll, I don't know
what's going on in that fucked up head of yours,
but having the police watching me like a hawk
has not been good for business."
He laughed in his maniacal way . . .
"Shit, babe . . . don't you know me?"

He brought his hand,
once a tool of the gods
that made music straight from heaven,
to her exposed throat.
"Yeah . . . you know me."
It took every ounce of will
for her to take his touch,
to not scream.

The odd push.
The odd slap.
Sometimes warranted,
sometimes begged for.
She was tougher,
he knew that.
Had the scars to prove it.
All out brawls.
Her always the victor,
if the term could apply
in such a state.
He didn't have the balls
to finish her.

His fingers pulsed against her neck,
flexing.
Flying back to his pocket
the second the door opened.

Fortitude

She cried that night.
cried for all the dreams
she never knew she was allowed to have . . .

For all the hurt
she confused with love.

For all the heart
she still had for life.

No pawns.
No excuses.
She had accepted her fate
without a fight,
but she had paid more dues than most.

Quiet and alone,
she moved closer to herself,
to the little girl
she had been so anxious to forget.

Life was not meant to be lived this way,
she knew that now.
Jane had been wrong.
She didn't "need" a man.
She had survived this long,
using,
abusing,

cruising,
toward . . .

A wake-up call.
A second chance
to stand as the woman
none would recognize.
The spirit she was born to be
would shine
brighter than any had ever believed.
She had been cast her lot,
but she did not have to accept it.

Homecoming

Balloons, so many balloons.
Silver and shiny,
hot-pink plastic,
yellow sunshine
to blind her fear.

Noon would be upon her soon.
Wheelchair bound,
but moving,
gliding through the corridors
that had been her home.

More of a home than Sal.
More of a home than her grandmother.
It saddened her to think
any human could be reduced
to such unholy standards.

For the first time in months
she was dressed
and ready to leave this behind.
She did not want to wait until noon.

Paperwork processed.
Just waiting for the ride.
It'll be off to Grandmother's house we go,
where Jane's abandoned room would be waiting,
along with the stained sheets
of sordid memories.

They would all be there
with more balloons.
Not the fancy helium-filled ones
bought to impress the nurses.

She knew her father's appearance
would not be enough
to warrant such extravagance.

She rolled on through the hallways,
smiling brightly
at the staff who knew nothing of her past,
who only judged her with pity
for a forgotten lifetime
and a crazy mother.

The mystery of the girl in room fifteen
would become legend.
Nurses would clamour for tales
on slow nightshifts,
over lunch
in the pastel pink cafeteria.

She smiled at the thought,
knowing
the mystery would soon be
about so much more than
who-done-it.

Ultimately,
it would be the mystery

of who-was-she
and how-did-she.

But no one
would ever have to question "why?"

A Mother's Wish

She had been lost
for so many years.

So lost.
She led her daughter
to the same dark nights of the soul.

And now this . . .

If a past could be forgotten,
the future could be rewritten.
The opportunity
to be the mother she never was,
to be the daughter she never was.

If her baby could live through this,
she could be the mother she needed,
the mother she wanted,
with no fear of hate,
of judgement.

The idea of the past
permanently buried,
the idea of a new start,
longing for those special moments
made for TV.

Sara took a deep breath.
She laughed to herself,
amazed at the nervousness she felt,
butterflies dancing.

Out of chaos,
out of pain,
love can surface.

The shame that had weighted her for so long,
that had kept her hateful,
like a wall between them.
Perhaps,
now,
the wall had crumbled.

They had talked.
They had laughed.
She shared happy moments
in tidbits only,
not wanting to bring it all back.
Coloring her past
with sunshine
and fluff,
not the stuff
it really was.

She put a nervous hand on the door knob,
still shocked at the excitement she felt
getting to bring her girl home.

She pulled the bouquet of balloons
tight into her tiny hands,
smiled her biggest smile,
and opened the door . . .

to an empty room.

Epilogue

:

For the Girl Who Used to Be

Here lie the fragments of a life laid to waste.
Bitterness, hate, the sour distaste.
Once blacked pieces of a once jaded heart
blown wide open by trust, by love . . . torn apart.

He whisked her away and buried her whole,
nurtured and cared, replanted her soul,
in earth that was primed with goodness and trust.
The past was the past, left there to rust.

With her heart firmly rooted, it blossomed too,
making new memories, old memories few.
Together they walked a path known by none.
For the first time in her life, near blinded by sun.

Letting go of them all, she found her way.
Risking a chance when he asked her to stay.
For the first time a home as was meant to be.
For the first time she learned, that she could love "me."

Settled In

He had never known the joy
of having someone waiting at home.
The other
had never been there.

She had twisted his heart,
the consequence
locked up tight,
so tight
no key would ever turn it
. . . or so he thought.

The tiny apartment,
once dark, depressing,
was alive now,
with light . . . with love.
Perhaps both
a result of the hope
that had suddenly blossomed.

Never had he been able to look toward the future,
never had he wanted to.
Resigned to a life alone.
The gridlock,
the grind,
he had accepted
it was a bed of his own making.

But sometimes,
destiny sets you on
a dark country road
in the wee hours of the morning,
in response to the call of a heart having given up.

And sometimes
when you stop to answer,
when you refuse to turn away
from the ugliness of the world,
her true beauty presents itself
in the mistreated heart
of another.

Five a.m. on a still dark morning.
He could see the light,
warm and welcoming,
shining from the tiny kitchen
through the mist of dawn.

She would be waiting,
she would be smiling.
He had given his notice
one week to go.

Then they would run . . .
like they had planned
all those weeks before.

When the police had landed,
this time he didn't mind the questions.

The answers had all been worked out,
and they were quick to leave him alone.

Physically, healing had been quick.
He believed there was even a chance
the internal bleeding
of a heart forever wasted,
had finally stopped.

He thought of her "parents,"
remembered the barely disguised relief
on the face of her father,
thought maybe for a moment
her mother was really concerned.

He shook his head,
pushing the reflections
back to the darkness.
If she could let go,
so could he.

He gave the ignition a twist.
Silencing the purr of the old Ford's engine,
his work boots pounded.
Stomp . . . stomp . . . stomp,
against the black top of the parking lot,
stomp . . . stomp . . . stomp.

His heart raced in anticipation,
pulse . . . pulse . . . pulse,
as he ran through the morning
to greet her.

About the Author

Natasha Head is a published poet who hails from the beautiful east coast of Canada. You can find her work in *Inspiration Speaks Volume 1*, and her debut collection, 2012 Pushcart Prize nominated *Nothing Left to Lose*, both available through Winter Goose Publishing. Her blog, tashtoo.com, is a vibrant example of her work in progress. She is also a proud Open-LinkNight host and resident tweeter for dVersePoets, and founding member of The New World Creative Union. Join her on BlogTalkRadio's The Creative Nexus each Thursday.

www.ingramcontent.com/pod-product-compliance
Lightning Source LLC
Chambersburg PA
CBHW070813050426
42452CB00011B/2024